Creature Comparisons

Bears

Tracey Crawford

Heinemann Library
Chicago, Illinois

Customer Service   888–454–2279

Visit our website at www.heinemannlibrary.com

Photo research by Tracy Cummins, Tracey Engel, and Ruth Blair
Designed by Jo Hinton-Malivoire
Printed and bound in China by South China Printing Company
10 09 08
10 9 8 7 6 5 4 3 2

Library of Congress Cataloging-in-Publication Data
Crawford, Tracey.
  Bears / Tracey Crawford.— 1st ed.
      p. cm. — (Creature comparisons)
  Includes bibliographical references and index.
  ISBN-13: 978-1-4034-8454-3 (hc) ISBN-10: 1-4034-8454-6 (hc)
  ISBN-13: 978-1-4034-8461-1 (pb) ISBN-10: 1-4034-8461-9 (pb)
  1. Bears—Juvenile literature. I. Title. II. Series.
  QL737.C27C735 2007
  599.78—dc22
                              2006007663

Acknowledgments
The author and publisher are grateful to the following for permission to reproduce copyright material: Alamy pp. **9** (John Schwieder), **10** (Garry DeLong), **13** (Balan), **17** (Winston Fraser); Corbis pp. **4** (bird, Arthur Morris), **5** (A. & S. Carey/zefa), **7** (Gunter Marx Photography), **14** (Ralph A. Clevenger), **15** (Keren Su), **18** (Michael DeYoung), **22** (polar bear, David E. Myers/zefa); Howie Garber p. **19**; Getty Images pp. **4** (fish), **6** (PhotoDisc), **11** (Roy Toft), **16** (Andy Rouse), **20** (Eastcott Momatiuk), **21** (Hans Strand); Naturepl.com p. **12**; Science Photo Library p. **22** (Sun bear, Art Wolfe); Carlton Ward p. **4** (snake, frog).

Cover photograph of a giant panda reproduced with permission of Corbis/Tim Davis and a brown bear reproduced with permission of Corbis/Royalty Free. Back cover photograph of a polar bear reproduced with permission of Corbis/Michael DeYoung.

Every effort has been made to contact copyright holders of any material reproduced in this book.
Any omissions will be rectified in subsequent printings if notice is given to the publisher.

Contents

There are many types of animals.

Bears are one type of animal.

All bears have fur.

All bears have paws and claws.

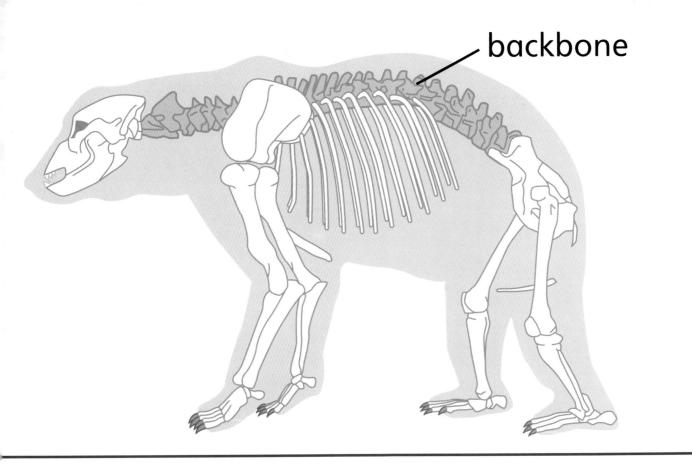

backbone

All bears have a backbone.

All baby bears get milk from their mother.

All bears walk on four legs.

All bears can stand on two feet.

Most bears sleep through the winter.

But this bear does not.

Some bears eat fish.

But these bears do not.

Some bears are big.

Some bears are small.

Some bears swim.

Some bears climb.

Every bear is different.

Every bear is special.

Bear Facts

Polar bears have two layers of fur. This helps keep them warm.

Sun bears spend most of their time in trees. They have long claws. This helps them climb.

Picture Glossary

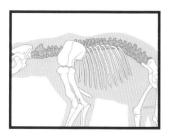 **backbone** the part of the skeleton that goes from the head to the tail

Index

Note to Parents and Teachers
In *Bears*, children are introduced to the diversity found within this animal group, as well as the characteristics that all bears share. The text has been carefully chosen with the advice of a literacy expert to enable beginning readers success while reading independently or with moderate support. Scientists were consulted to provide both interesting and accurate content.

By showing the importance of diversity within wildlife, *Bears* invites children to welcome diversity in their own lives. The book ends by stating that every bear is a unique, special creature. Use this as a discussion point for how each person is also unique and special. You can support children's nonfiction literacy skills by helping them to use the table of contents, picture glossary, and index.